Bobby Shaftoe, clap your hands

Musical fun with new songs from old favourites

Sue Nicholls

**with illustrations by Lynn Breeze
Cover by Alex Ayliffe**

A&C Black • London

Introduction

For Rebecca Davies who
loved music

First published 1992 by
A & C Black (Publishers) Ltd
35 Bedford Row
London WC1R 4JH

Reprinted 1993, 1994, 1997.
Text © 1992 Sue Nicholls
Inside illustrations © 1992
Lynne Breeze
Cover illustration © 1992
Alex Ayliffe
Design by Janet Watson
Edited by Sheena Roberts
Typeset by
Seton Music Graphics Ltd, Eire
Printed in Great Britain by
Martins the Printers Ltd
Berwick upon Tweed

ISBN 0 7136 3556 8

Bobby Shaftoe, clap your hands is a collection of new songs created from favourite playgroup, nursery and infant school melodies. New melodies can be difficult to pick up if you are not a fluent music reader — this book offers a wealth of new material using the melodies you already know and can confidently sing with your children.

Each song has been carefully devised to help you develop your children's musical skills. The four sections cover a wide range of activities, and will be particularly helpful in establishing the groundwork of the National Curriculum in Music:

SECTION ONE — Actions, movement and imagination
Hand, and whole-body actions and movement help children to improve their physical co-ordination, and their ability to 'feel' music's pulse. This section also offers many opportunities for adding new verses, and using voices as well as bodies expressively.

SECTION TWO — Exploring sounds
The new songs in this section give opportunities for selecting, handling, and playing instruments in a controlled manner. Vocal, body and environmental sounds are explored as well.

SECTION THREE — Listening songs
Careful, discriminative listening is essential if children are to learn how to select and use sounds for themselves. Through experiencing a range of sounds — heard singly, in combination, and at different volumes — they develop a sound palette to use in their own compositions.

SECTION FOUR — Making patterns
The activities in these songs demand a finer control of sounds — playing on the strong beats, or in the rhythm of the words, or keeping silent until it is your turn to play.

About the melodies

It is unlikely that any of the melodies will be unfamiliar to you; but just as a word you want to use can be on the tip of your tongue, so can a melody momentarily escape you. To prod your memory the first few notes of each song are given on the page in letter names. You can use chime bars, a xylophone or glockenspiel to play them. These are the notes you will need:

B, C D E F G A B C' D'

(The dash below the letter B indicates the note below C. The dashes above indicate high C and high D.)

If any song is unknown to you, you will find the melody written out at the back of the book. Find someone who reads music to teach it to you. (You may know a different version of the tune, but the words will fit whichever version you know so don't be afraid to use it.)

The melodies at the back are all given in a range suitable for children's voices. Wherever possible the chime bar letter names are the same, but in a very few cases in order to avoid a ♭ or ♯ note, they are in a different range.

No accompaniment, other than that which you and the children create using your classroom instruments, is necessary when singing the songs together. A piano can be more of a hindrance than a help when singing with young children. A light guitar accompaniment can be useful occasionally and guitar chords are given with the melodies — but your own unaccompanied voice is all that the children really need. Your hands are then free to show them actions, and you can concentrate your attention fully on how the children are responding.

You will find there are many suggestions for developing the songs further, but you can use your own and your children's ideas to take them further still.

Sue Nicholls

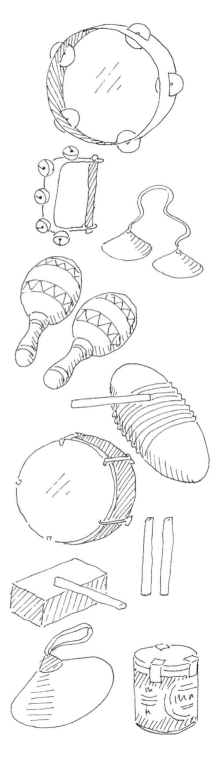

Contents

SECTION THREE – Listening songs

SECTION FOUR – Making patterns

1 Welcome song

Tune: My hat it has three corners

Let's say hello to Jamey,
Let's say hello to Ruth,
Let's say hello to Suresh,
They're welcome here today.

Sit in a circle and welcome each child in turn.
Change the words to incorporate actions if
you like:

Let's wave hello to Christine . . .

We'll clap our hands for Dorothy . . .

   G C' G G E F D
Let's say hello to Jamey

2 Monday's here
Tune: This old man

Monday's here,
Monday's here,
Monday's here, now is that clear?
Do a puzzle, wouldn't that be fun?
Lots to do for everyone.

As the song progresses through the week, the children can suggest different activities for each day, e.g.

Paint a picture . . .
We can dress up . . .
Find the brick box . . .

G E   G   G E G
Monday's here, Monday's here

3 What is the weather today?

Tune: Hickory dickory dock

Leader: What is the weather today?
All: What is the weather today?
Leader: It's warm and dry,
All: It's warm and dry,
All: That is the weather today.

Change lines three and four to suit the weather:

What is the weather today?
What is the weather today?
It's cold and wet,
It's cold and wet,
That is the weather today.

Change it to what you can do in different kinds of weather:

Leader: Now we can go out to play,
All: Now we can go out to play,
Leader: It's warm and dry,
All: It's warm and dry,
All: Now we can go out to play.

We can wear wellington boots,
We can wear wellington boots,
It's cold and wet,
It's cold and wet,
We can wear wellington boots.

To make it a longer activity, put pictures of different kinds of weather into a box. The child who dips into the box decides on an appropriate line to sing, and may choose to sing that line alone, echoed by the group. Alternatively, the leader can sing the child's idea.

E F G G A B C'
What is the weather today?

4 What is yellow?

Tune: Frère Jacques

Leader:	What is yellow?
All:	What is yellow?
Leader:	Can you tell?
All:	Can you tell?
Leader:	Daffodils and sunshine,
All:	Daffodils and sunshine,
Leader:	Lemons as well,
All:	Lemons as well.

What is green?
What is green?
Can you tell?
Can you tell?
Shuma's brand new anorak,
Shuma's brand new anorak,
Grass as well,
Grass as well.

Before starting the song talk about things which are yellow and decide which ones to include. Sing the song then choose another colour.

Variations

Explore properties other than colour, e.g.

What is dangerous?
What is smooth?
What is hollow? etc.

F G A F   F G A F
What is yellow, what is yellow

5 Make a cake

Tune: Simple Simon

We can make a cake for tea,
But what shall we put in it?
Flour and eggs and milk and jam,
We'll bake it in a minute.

Vary the ingredients in line three – the children will enjoy thinking up new ones. Unlikely or revolting items are always popular! e.g.

Spiders, worms and glue and string.

Variations

We can make a spell today (Hallowe'en)
Let us make a cake for Pete (Birthday)

F F G A F F E
We can make a cake for tea

6 I'm walking like a robot
Tune: Poor Jenny sits a-weeping

I'm walking like a robot, a robot, a robot,
I'm walking like a robot, all metal and wires.

My arms move very stiffly, very stiffly, very stiffly,
My arms move very stiffly, when I brush my teeth.

My head can turn quite quickly, quite quickly, quite quickly,
My head can turn quite quickly, with a hum and a click.

My chest is full of buttons, full of buttons, full of buttons,
My chest is full of buttons, they go bleep, bleep, blip.

Do the actions indicated by the words and add new verses with the
children's suggestions.

D   G   A   B   C' D' B
I'm walking like a robot

7 Don't drop litter!

Tune: Ten green bottles

Don't drop litter – put it in the bin!
Don't drop litter – put it in the bin!
Let's keep our playground tidy, neat and clean,
So don't drop litter – put it in the bin!

No crisp packets – put them in the bin!
No crisp packets – put them in the bin!
Let's keep our playground tidy, neat and clean,
So no crisp packets – put them in the bin.

Additional verses can be suggested by the children substituting other types of litter for crisp packets. The repeated line *put it in the bin* can be supported effectively with claves, sticks or actions.

G   G G B A G A B G
Don't drop litter – Put it in the bin!

8 Witch's song

Tune: Baa baa black sheep

Witch's cauldron,

 Here's the witch's hat,

Witch's broomstick,

 Witch's cat,

Fly over here,

 Fly over there,

Crash, Bang, Alazam!

 Now you disappear.

Witch's spider,

Crawling up a log,

Witch's spell book,

Witch's frog,

Hop over here,

Hop over there,

Crash, Bang, Alazam!

Now you disappear.

C C G G A B C' A G
Witch's cauldron, Here's the witch's hat

9 A feely game

Tune: Little brown jug

Here's a bag to feel inside,
Something's there that likes to hide.
Hard or soft, large or small,
Can you guess its name at all?

To play this game you need a fabric bag with an elasticated opening.
Secretly place a small toy (or any object capable of being identified
by touch) in the bag and pass it around the ring during the song. The
child holding the bag at the end slips his or her hand in and, without
looking, tries to identify the object by feeling it.

You could hide: a coin, toothbrush, spoon, marble, key, ring, etc.

E G G G F A A
Here's a bag to feel inside

10 Here's a flapping ghost

Tune: Row, row, row your boat

Here's a flapping ghost,
Sitting down to tea!
Ooh, ooh, ooh, ooh!
Save a cake for me.

Here's a flapping ghost,
Sitting down to lunch!
Ooh, ooh, ooh, ooh!
What is there to munch?

Here's a flapping ghost,
Sitting down to dine!
Ooh, ooh, ooh, ooh!
I shall stay 'til nine!

The children can make flapping arm movements during the song and a small group can select instruments to accompany the *oohs* to give a spooky effect.

C C C D   E   E D   E F G
Here's a flapping ghost, Sitting down to tea!

11 Spaceship to the moon

Tune: John Brown's body

Shuma has a spaceship that will take us to the moon,
Shuma has a spaceship that will take us to the moon,
Shuma has a spaceship that will take us to the moon,
So we climb in, press the switch, and zoom.
    We can walk around in moonboots,
    We can walk around in moonboots,
    We can walk around in moonboots,
    We're walking on the moon.

David has a spaceship that will take us to the moon . . .
    We can ride off in our buggy,
    We can ride off in our buggy,
    We can ride off in our buggy,
    We're riding on the moon.

Sally has a spaceship that will take us to the moon . . .
    We can jump around in craters,
    We can jump around in craters,
    We can jump around in craters,
    We're jumping on the moon.

D D D C B, D G A B B B A G
Shuma has a spaceship that will take us to the moon

Ask the children
for ideas for
more verses.

12 Oh, can you stand on one leg?

Tune: Aiken Drum

Oh, can you stand on one leg,
On one leg, on one leg?
Oh, can you stand on one leg
And hop around the room?

Oh, can you stand on two legs,
On two legs, on two legs?
Now can you stand on two legs
And jump around the room?

Oh, can you stand on ten toes,
On ten toes, on ten toes?
Oh, can you stand on ten toes
And tiptoe round the room?

Oh, can you stand on hands and feet,
On hands and feet, on hands and feet,
Oh, can you stand on hands and feet
And be an elephant?

G E E E C F F
Oh, can you stand on one leg

13 Tiny caterpillar

Tune: She'll be coming round the mountain

There's a tiny caterpillar on a leaf, wiggle wiggle,
There's a tiny caterpillar on a leaf, wiggle wiggle,
There's a tiny caterpillar, tiny caterpillar,
There's a tiny caterpillar on a leaf, wiggle wiggle.

He will eat the leaves around him 'til he's full,
  munch munch . . .

A cocoon is what he's spinning for his home,
  spin spin . . .

Then he'll be a butterfly and flap away,
   flap flap . . .

So that tiny caterpillar went like this,
   wiggle wiggle, munch munch, spin spin,
   flap flap . . .

D   EGG G G E D B, D G
There's a tiny caterpillar on a leaf

This song will make an
excellent partner to Eric
Carle's classic story. *The
very hungry caterpillar.*

14 Choose an instrument

Tune: London Bridge

Choose an instrument you can play,
You can play, you can play,
Choose an instrument you can play,
What's your favourite?

Sanjay plays the tambourine,
Tambourine, tambourine,
Sanjay plays the tambourine,
That's his favourite.

The children sit in a circle with a selection of percussion instruments in the centre. A beanbag is passed round while everyone sings the first verse. Whoever holds the bean bag at the end, chooses an instrument and plays it while everyone sings the second verse. The child returns to his or her place and the game begins again.

Variation

Older children can sing the second verse as a solo:

I can play the tambourine . . .

    G   A G G   F   E   F   G
Choose an instrument you can play

15 Bang, bang, the sticks go bang

Tune: Tom, Tom, the piper's son

Bang, bang, the sticks go bang!
Play as loudly as you can,
Now as quietly as a mouse,
Creeping softly round the house.

Everyone has a pair of sticks or claves. (Sawn-off lengths of broomhandle are cheap and make a reasonable sound.) The children match the volume of their playing to the words of the song.

G   G   A   B   G   G
Bang, bang, the sticks go bang

Variations

Change to tambourines, shakers, a body or vocal sound.

16 A dragon's very fierce
Tune: The grand old Duke of York

Oh, a dragon's very fierce,
A dragon's very tough,
And when he breathes out orange fire
The smoke comes out in puffs!
His scales are shining green,
They make a rattling sound,
His feet go stomp,
His teeth go chomp,
His tail thumps on the ground.

Talk about the words of the song. What sounds
do they suggest? Let the children experiment with
instruments and other sound sources to use as they
sing the song. Here are some ideas: *crackling flames* –
plastic chocolate tray; *scales* – squashed drink cans rattled
together; *chomping teeth* – ridged plastic bottle scraped
with a pencil.

Variation

Simply use body and vocal sounds, e.g.
rub nails together for *scales*, blow for smoke-puffs and use
stamping and banging on the floor for *stomp* and *thumps*.

B A G D B D G
Oh, a dragon's very fierce

17 A hedgehog is very prickly

Tune: One finger, one thumb, keep moving

A hedgehog is very prickly,
A hedgehog is very prickly,
A hedgehog is very prickly,
It couldn't be anything else.

Once the general idea has been grasped, children will enjoy adding new verses and appropriate body or vocal sounds as well as actions.

A fish is very slippery,
A fish is very slippery,
A fish is very slippery,
It couldn't be anything else.

A crocodile's very snappy . . .

A crab is very nippy . . .

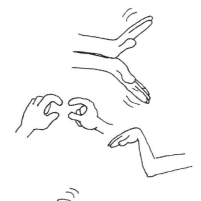

A snake is very hissy . . .

A worm is very wiggly . . .

Variation

Talk about the instruments you might use to accompany each verse. What kind of sounds are suggested by a word like *prickly* – would they be long or short, loud or quiet, gentle or harsh.

C F F F F F F C
A hedgehog is very prickly

18 A monster came to visit you!

Tune: The animals went in two by two

A monster came to visit you.
  He roared! He roared!
A monster came to visit you.
  He roared! He roared!
A monster came to visit you,
His head was green and his nose was too,
You could hear him roaring,
Did he frighten you? No! *(Shout)*

Change *He roared* to *He hissed*, *He snarled*, or *He grunted*. These sound words may be accompanied with instruments – talk about the sounds the children would like to use. They might find home-made instruments effective – try tins filled with sand or gravel, scrunchy packaging, ripped newspaper, cardboard rolls for roaring through, and so on.

roar
roar

E E A   A   B C'B C'   A   G   E G
A monster came to visit you, he roared, he roared

Before repeating the song, someone in the group can choose a new monster colour to substitute for green.

19 Postman's knocking

Tune: Polly put the kettle on

Postman's knocking rat-tat-tat,
Postman's knocking rat-tat-tat,
Postman's knocking rat-tat-tat,
He's at your door.

(Mark takes a toy car out of the sack.)

Mark's car goes brrrm brrrm brrrm,
Mark's car goes brrrm brrrm brrrm,
Mark's car goes brrrm brrrm brrrm,
When he plays.

Postman's knocking rat-tat-tat . . .

(Lloyd picks out a plastic bottle.)

Lloyd's bottle goes foo foo foo,
Lloyd's bottle goes foo foo foo,
Lloyd's bottle goes foo foo foo,
When he blows.

The children sit in a circle, each with a pair of claves or sticks. A 'postman' is chosen, who carries a sack containing small objects which suggest sounds (for instance, a toy car, aeroplane, or animal) or with which a sound can be made (for instance, an empty plastic bottle, a couple of yoghurt pots, etc.).

During the first verse, the postman walks around the outside of the circle. When *rat-tat-tat* is sung, everyone plays that pattern on their sticks.

On the word *door* the postman offers his sack to the nearest child, who picks something from the sack, without looking. The child thinks of a sound that his or her chosen object can make, and everyone sings the second verse.

The child returns the toy to the sack and becomes the postman.

G   A   G   F E C C
Postman's knocking rat-tat-tat

20 The hammers bang

Tune: I saw three ships

The hammers bang on my machine,
On my machine, on my machine,
The hammers bang on my machine,
They work from morning 'til evening.

The levers clang on my machine,
On my machine, on my machine,
The levers clang on my machine,
They work from morning 'til evening.

The lights all flash on my machine,
On my machine, on my machine,
The lights all flash on my machine,
They work from morning 'til evening.

The cutters snip on my machine,
On my machine, on my machine,
The cutters snip on my machine,
They work from morning 'til evening.

The metal goes crunch on my machine,
On my machine, on my machine,
The metal goes crunch on my machine,
It works from morning 'til evening.

The oil goes slurp on my machine,
On my machine, on my machine,
The oil goes slurp on my machine,
It works from morning 'til evening.

C F F G A C' A G
The hammers bang on my machine

Talk about the various sound possibilities before singing this song. The machine parts and their sounds can be varied – the children's experience and vocabulary will dictate the number of verses tackled.

Build up an accompaniment for each verse using the instruments the children choose. You might ask them to play *just* on the sound words – *bang*, *flash*, *snip*, etc. – or they might keep up a regular beat throughout. If you can stand the volume, allow the children to accumulate the sounds verse by verse.

It is an ideal song for including less conventional instruments, for example, a wonderful *crunch* can be achieved by using the plastic trays from chocolate or biscuit boxes, and plastic bottles containing a little water will produce excellent *slurps* when shaken.

21 I have sounds, one and two

Tune: Tommy thumb

I have sounds, one and two,
Hide away!
Listen now, carefully!
Which shall I play?

Introduce two *dissimilar*-sounding instruments to the children. Hide them behind a screen or in a box, and at the end of the song, play *one* of them. The children must rely solely on the sound they hear to identify the instrument.

When the children can distinguish two very different sounds easily, either use pairs of *similar*-sounding instruments (e.g. triangle and indian bells) or increase the number of sounds in the game:

I have sounds, one, two, three . . .
I have sounds, there are four . . .

E F   G   E F   G   A C' G
I have sounds one and two, Hide away!

22 Musical box

Tune: Here we go looby loo

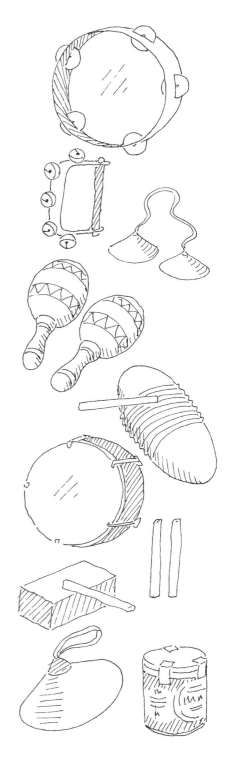

Musical box goes round,
Musical box goes round,
Musical box goes round and round,
What will it tell you to play?

Musical box goes round,
Musical box goes round,
Musical box goes round and round,
That's what it told you to play.

Prepare small cards with simple drawings of your instruments. These are put into a 'musical box' which is passed around the ring while the children sing the song. The child holding the box at the end dips in, takes a card and finds the appropriate instrument from the centre of the circle. He or she plays while the song is sung again. Put the card and instrument back to ensure that there are always enough to give several turns.

C C C   E   C   G   C C C   E   C   D
Musical box goes round, Musical box goes round

23 Drummer in the ring

Tune: The farmer's in his den

The drummer's in the ring,
The drummer's in the ring.
Is he loud or is he quiet?
The drummer's in the ring.

E G G A A G
The drummer's in the ring

A child with a drum walks around the inside of a ring of children, playing loudly or quietly while they sing the song. When the song ends, the nearest child to the drummer says whether he or she thinks the sound was loud or quiet. The child who guesses becomes the new drummer, and the game begins again.

If the drummer's sound is ambiguous, ask him or her to play two sounds – one loud, one soft. The listening child can be asked to say which is the loud sound.

24 Listen, children

Tune: Mary, Mary, quite contrary

Leader: Listen, children, here by the window,
What sounds can you hear?
Solo: I heard a car,
All: We heard a car,
All: Now what will the next sound be?

A song for listening carefully to environmental sounds. Pause to listen after *What sounds can you hear?* and let the children take turns to sing about what they heard. Different places can be substituted for *here by the window*, e.g.

Listen, children, here in the playground/kitchen/classroom . . .

You can also prepare a tape of environmental sounds for the children to identify, or play instrumental sounds behind a screen:

Listen, children, listen very closely . . .

D' D' B B C' B C' A A
Listen, children, here by the window

25 Mrs Bear

Tune: Oats and beans and barley grow

Mrs Bear lives in a cave,
Mrs Bear lives in a cave,
Now who will dare, now who will dare
To steal a sound from Mrs Bear?

Sit the children in a ring. Select two instruments and make sure that the children know their names and sounds. Mrs Bear is chosen. She sits in the circle and the two instruments are placed just behind her so that she cannot see them.

A card with a mask drawn on it (to suggest a thief) is passed around the ring while the song is sung. The child holding the card at the end goes behind Mrs Bear and places the card by one instrument, thus stealing it. The thief then plays that instrument and Mrs Bear must guess its name. The thief becomes Mrs Bear and the game continues.

G G E C F A G
Missis Bear lives in a cave

26 Make your sound like mine

Tune: Do you know the muffin man?

Make your sound as quiet as mine,
As quiet as mine,
As quiet as mine.
Make your sound as quiet as mine,
And do it after me!

The children and leader
sing the verse together.
At the end the leader uses
his or her hands to make
a quiet sound which the
children then copy.

Variations

loud – clap
long – rub palms together
short – tap or click
fast – pat knees quickly

D G G A B G G
Make your sound as quiet as mine

27 Some sounds are short

Tune: Pease pudding hot

Some sounds are short,
Some sounds are long,
Which sound will you make
After this song?

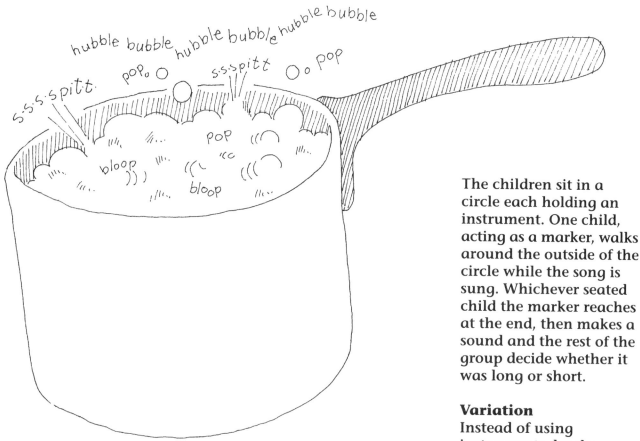

The children sit in a circle each holding an instrument. One child, acting as a marker, walks around the outside of the circle while the song is sung. Whichever seated child the marker reaches at the end, then makes a sound and the rest of the group decide whether it was long or short.

Variation
Instead of using instruments, let the children make up long and short vocal or body sounds.

C   C   D   E   E   F   F   F   E

Some sounds are short, Some sounds are long

28 One sound can be heard

Tune: One man went to mow

One sound can be heard,
When we sing together.
One sound can be heard,
When we sing together.

Two sounds can be heard,
When we sing together,
Two sounds can be heard,
When we sing together.

Select *three* instruments that sound unalike, and introduce them to the children. Devise a means of hiding the instruments with a screen or box, and play one of them while everyone sings the first part. At the end, the children say which one was played. During the second part, the teacher plays the *first* instrument and *one* of the others. The children then say what they think the additional sound was.

By hiding *three* instruments, the second sound is not automatically guessed: to identify it the children must really listen.

You can increase the number of hidden sounds with older children.

E   E   E   E   E   E   E   F   E   E   D

One sound can be heard, When we sing together

29 Clap your hands and wiggle your fingers

Tune: Bobby Shaftoe

Clap your hands and wiggle your fingers,
Clap your hands and wiggle your fingers,
Clap your hands and wiggle your fingers,
  Now we've made a pattern.

Tap your knees and blink your eye-lids,
Tap your knees and blink your eye-lids,
Tap your knees and blink your eye-lids,
  Now we've made a pattern.

Bang the floor and nod your head,
Bang the floor and nod your head,
Bang the floor and nod your head,
  Now we've made a pattern.

Rub your hands and shake your shoulders,
Rub your hands and shake your shoulders,
Rub your hands and shake your shoulders,
  Now we've made a pattern.

G   G   G   C' B B D' B G
Clap your hands and wiggle your fingers

Each verse introduces a new pattern of actions: one action produces a *sound* and the other is *silent*.

Can the children think of more sounds and silent actions to add?

30 Hold a stick in this hand

Tune: Sing a song of sixpence

Hold a stick in this hand,
Hold a stick in that,
Put them both together,
Let them tap, tap, tap.
Tap them near the ceiling,
Tap them near the ground,
Tap them just in front of you,
Then gently put them down.

C' B A G C' E
Hold a stick in this hand

Everyone has a pair of
sticks or claves placed
on the ground in front of
them (as a knife and fork
might be) before the song
starts. They pick them up
and play them as the
words direct.

31 Clap hands, follow me

Tune: Skip to my loo

Clap hands, follow me,
Clap hands, follow me,
Clap hands, follow me,
Who will be leader next time?

Stamp feet, follow Jane,
Stamp feet, follow Jane,
Stamp feet, follow Jane,
Who will be leader next time?

Jump high, follow Gita,
Jump high, follow Gita,
Jump high, follow Gita,
Who will be leader next time?

Sing this as a follow-my-leader with the one who suggests the new action leading the line round the room, marching or dancing.

If the song is sung sitting down, let the child who thinks up the action stand up and lead from his or her place.

E   C   E E G
Clap hands, follow me

32 Hand upon your head

Tune: Jelly on the plate

Hand upon your head,
Hand upon your head,
Up and down, up and down,
Hand upon your head.

Elbow on your knee,
Elbow on your knee,
Change it over, change it over,
Elbow on your knee.

Foot upon the floor,
Foot upon the floor,
Slide it round, slide it round,
Foot upon the floor.

E G G G G   F A A A A
Hand upon your head, Hand upon your head

The children can have
fun thinking of more
actions to perform – see if
they can find some really
tricky ones.

33 Round the ring

Tune: Here we go round the mulberry bush

Sophie is walking round the ring,
Round the ring, round the ring,
Sophie is walking round the ring,
What will she choose to play?

Sophie can play and so can we,
Sophie can play and so can we,
Sophie can play and so can we,
Time to choose a new leader.

The children sit in a circle with a selection of instruments in the centre. Everyone has a pair of sticks. A child (Sophie) is chosen to walk around the inside of the circle while everyone sings the first verse.

Once Sophie has selected an instrument, she returns to her place ready for the second verse. Whenever the words *Sophie can play* are sung, Sophie plays alone, but on *and so can we* everyone else plays their sticks.

Young children may not be able to produce the precise rhythm of the words and this will not detract from the song in any way, but it is a useful exercise to be able to keep to a general pattern of solo/group/solo/group, and to learn to listen to the two distinct instrumental sounds played during the song.

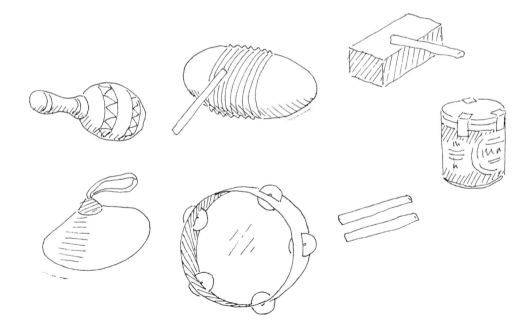

G G G G B D' B G
Sophie is walking round the ring

34 Stick-tapping

Tune: The wheels on the bus

We're tapping a pattern with the sticks,

With the sticks, with the sticks,

We're tapping a pattern with the sticks,

   While we sing.

A simple song to encourage children to keep up an instrumental pattern as they sing. If the group plays on the underlined syllables, they will be marking the pulse or beat of the song, but many patterns would fit, e.g.

simply follow the pattern of the words by tapping on every syllable:
We're tapping a pattern with the sticks

just play on *with the sticks*

allow the children to play their own patterns at random during the song, or take turns to play while the others sing.

Variation

Divide the children into groups, each group playing a different kind of instrument. Make up verses for each group to play, e.g.

Corrugated card: *we're scraping a pattern on the card*
Hands: *we're clapping a pattern with our hands*
Bells: *we're shaking a pattern with the bells*

   G   A   G   G   F   D   C   E   E
We're tapping a pattern with the sticks

35 Tap your name

Tune: Hot cross buns

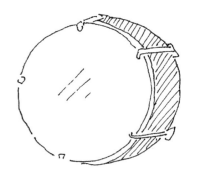

Tap your name,
Tap your name,
Pass the tambour round the ring,
And tap your name.
Who will have the next go?
Can you play the game?
Pass the tambour round the ring,
And tap your name.

The children sit in a circle and pass round a tambour while they sing the song. The child holding it at the end, taps his or her name. First names will be complex enough for very young children – older children can tap out their second name as well.

After a few turns, stop the game to ask questions about the patterns in the names, e.g.

Has anyone tapped a name with the same pattern as Shuma? (Peter, Sally, Sejal)

How many taps were there in Jeremy's name?

Variation

Change tambour to drum, woodblock, etc.

C'   C   F   C'   C   F
Tap your name, Tap your name

36 I can play you my sound

Tune: Ring a ring o' roses

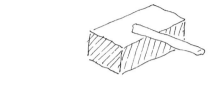

Leader: I can play you my sound,
Children: I can play you my sound,
Leader: I play,
Children: I play,
All: We all play now.

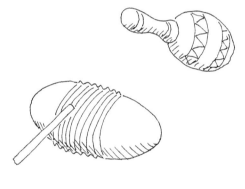

Give each child in the group a different instrument. The leader sings the first line whilst playing his or her instrument. The children echo this with their instruments, singing the same words. The next two lines follow the same pattern and on the final line everyone sings and plays together.

Variation

Let everyone pass their instrument to the left before starting the song again.

E E D F E C
I can play you my sound

37 Do you know the colours?

Tune: Oranges and lemons

Do you know the colours
That you find in a rainbow?
Do you know the colours
When the sun and rain meet?
   Red, orange, yellow,
   Then green and blue follow,
   Indigo, violet,
   And the pattern's complete.
You know the colours
That you find in a rainbow,
You know the colours
When the sun and rain meet.

With young children, talk about the sounds they could make to represent sunshine and raindrops. They might like the sound of drumming their palms lightly on their knees for raindrops, whereas the warmth of the sun might be represented by the low notes of a xylophone. Once they have selected their sounds, help them devise a sequence, for instance:

sun sounds →
rain sounds →
rain and sun together →
sun sounds

Older children might try making a pattern of colours, using instrumental sounds to describe them. This will involve discussion with the children about the sounds they associate with the colours. There are no rights or wrongs, and choices may be entirely personal.

C' C' A C' A F
Do you know the colours

38 Goodbye song
Tune: My hat it has three corners

Let's say goodbye to Amil,
Let's say goodbye to Janet,
Let's say goodbye to Timothy,
We've had a lovely play.

Use in the same way as the *Welcome Song*.

G C' G G E F D
Let's say goodbye to Amil

Melody lines

1 Welcome song - My hat it has three corners (also **38 Goodbye song**)

Let's say hel - lo to Ja - mey,____ Let's say hel - lo to Ruth,____ Let's

say hel - lo to Su - resh,____ They're wel - come here to - day.____

2 Monday's here - This old man

Mon - day's here, Mon - day's here, Mon - day's here, now is that clear?

Do a puz - zle, would - n't that be fun? Lots to do for eve - ry - one.

3 What is the weather today? - Hickory dickory dock

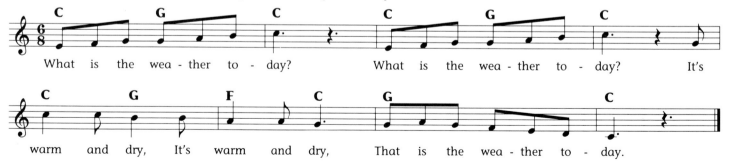

What is the wea - ther to - day? What is the wea - ther to - day? It's

warm and dry, It's warm and dry, That is the wea - ther to - day.

4 What is yellow? - Frère Jacques

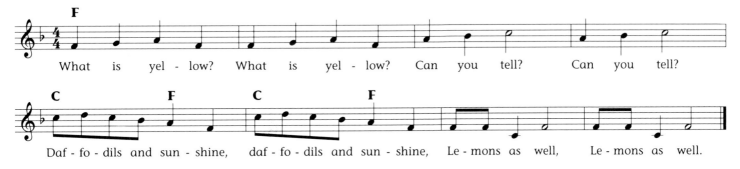

What is yel - low? What is yel - low? Can you tell? Can you tell?

Daf - fo - dils and sun - shine, daf - fo - dils and sun - shine, Le - mons as well, Le - mons as well.

5 Make a cake - Simple Simon

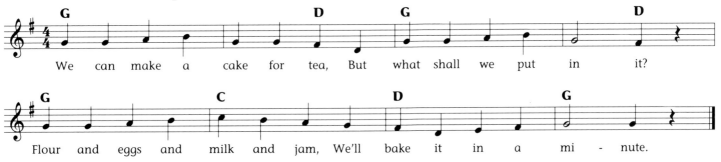

We can make a cake for tea, But what shall we put in it?

Flour and eggs and milk and jam, We'll bake it in a mi - nute.

6 I'm walking like a robot - Poor Jenny is a-weeping

I'm walk - ing like a ro - bot, a ro - bot, a ro - bot, I'm

walk - ing like a ro - bot, all me - tal and wires.

7 Don't drop litter! - Ten green bottles

Don't drop lit - ter, ___ put it in the bin! Don't drop lit - ter, ___

put it in the bin! Let's keep our play - ground ti - dy, neat and clean, So

don't drop lit - ter, ___ put it in the bin.

8 Witch's song - Baa baa black sheep

Wit - ch's caul - dron, Here's the wit - ch's hat, Wit - ch's broom - stick, Wit - ch's cat,

Fly o - ver here, Fly o - ver there, Crash, Bang, A - la - zam! Now you dis - ap - pear.

9 A feely game - Little brown jug

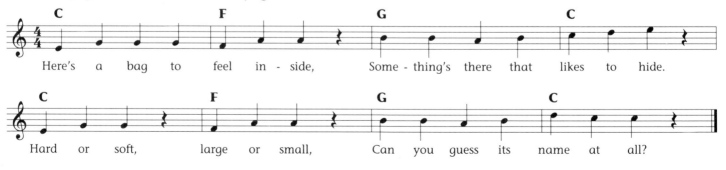

Here's a bag to feel in - side, Some - thing's there that likes to hide.

Hard or soft, large or small, Can you guess its name at all?

10 Here's a flapping ghost - Row, row, row your boat

Here's a flap - ping ghost, Sit - ting down to tea!

Ooh, ooh, ooh, ooh! Save a cake for me.

11 Spaceship to the moon - John Brown's body

Shu - ma has a space - ship that will take us to the moon, Shu - ma has a space - ship that will

take us to the moon, Shu - ma has a space - ship that will take us to the moon, So we

climb in, press the switch, and zoom. We can walk a - round in moon - boots,

We can walk a - round in moon - boots, We can walk a - round in

moon - boots, We're walk - ing on the moon.

12 Oh, can you stand on one leg? - Aiken Drum

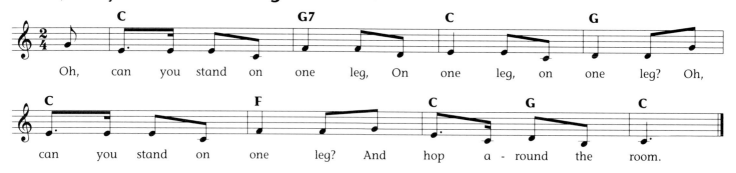

Oh, can you stand on one leg, On one leg, on one leg? Oh, can you stand on one leg? And hop a - round the room.

13 Tiny caterpillar - She'll be coming round the mountain

There's a ti - ny ca - ter - pil - lar on a leaf, wig - gle wig - gle, There's a ti - ny ca - ter - pil - lar on a leaf, wig - gle wig - gle, There's a ti - ny ca - ter - pil - lar, Ti - ny ca - ter - pil - lar, Ti - ny ca - ter - pil - lar on a leaf, wig - gle wig - gle.

14 Choose an instrument - London Bridge

Choose an in - stru - ment you can play, you can play, you can play,

Choose an in - stru - ment you can play, What's your fa - vourite?

15 Bang, bang, the sticks go bang - Tom, Tom, the piper's son

Bang, bang, the sticks go bang! Play as loud - ly____ as you can,

Now as quiet - ly as a mouse, Creep - ing____ soft - ly round the house.

16 A dragon's very fierce - The grand old Duke of York

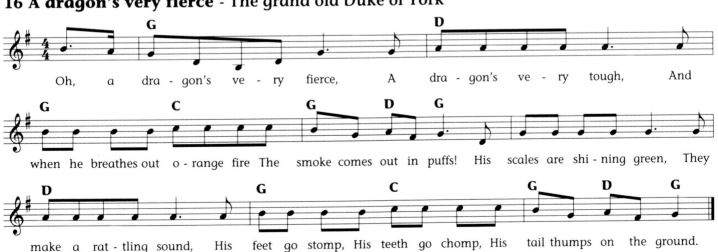

Oh, a dra - gon's ve - ry fierce, A dra - gon's ve - ry tough, And

when he breathes out o - range fire The smoke comes out in puffs! His scales are shi - ning green, They

make a rat - tling sound, His feet go stomp, His teeth go chomp, His tail thumps on the ground.

17 A hedgehog is very prickly - One finger, one thumb, keep moving

A hedge-hog is ve-ry prick-ly, A hedge-hog is ve-ry prick-ly, A hedge-hog is ve-ry prick-ly, It could-n't be a-ny-thing else.

18 A monster came to visit you! - The animals went in two by two

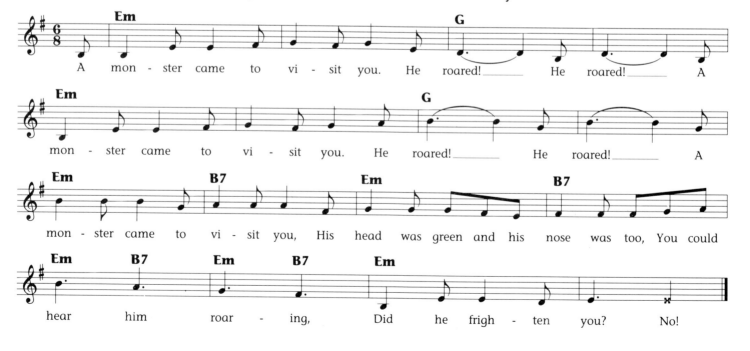

A mon-ster came to vi-sit you. He roared! He roared! A mon-ster came to vi-sit you. He roared! He roared! A mon-ster came to vi-sit you, His head was green and his nose was too, You could hear him roar-ing, Did he frigh-ten you? No!

19 Postman's knocking - Polly put the kettle on

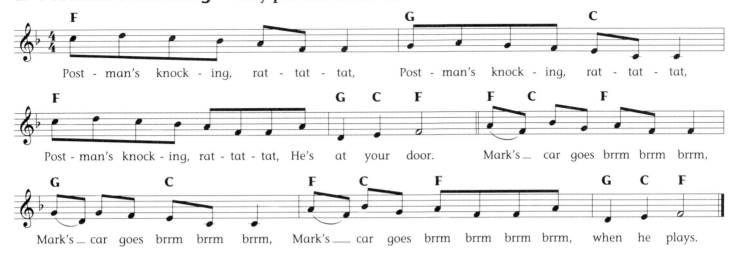

Post - man's knock - ing, rat - tat - tat, Post - man's knock - ing, rat - tat - tat,

Post - man's knock - ing, rat - tat - tat, He's at your door. Mark's _ car goes brrm brrm brrm,

Mark's _ car goes brrm brrm brrm, Mark's _ car goes brrm brrm brrm brrm, when he plays.

20 The hammers bang on my machine - I saw three ships

The ham - mers bang on my ma - chine, On my ma - chine, on my ma - chine, The

ham - mers bang on my ma - chine, They work from mor - ning 'til eve - ning.

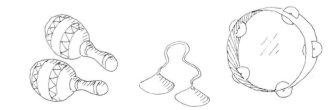

21 I have sounds one and two - Tommy thumb

I have sounds one and two, Hide a - way! Lis - ten now, care - ful - ly! Which shall I play?

22 Musical box - Here we go looby loo

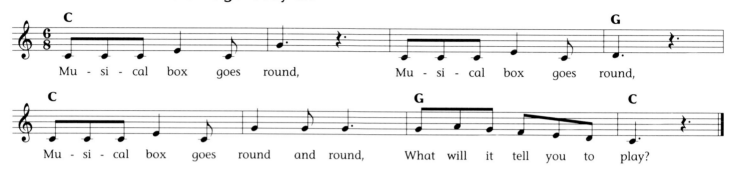

Mu - si - cal box goes round, Mu - si - cal box goes round,

Mu - si - cal box goes round and round, What will it tell you to play?

23 Drummer in the ring - The farmer's in his den

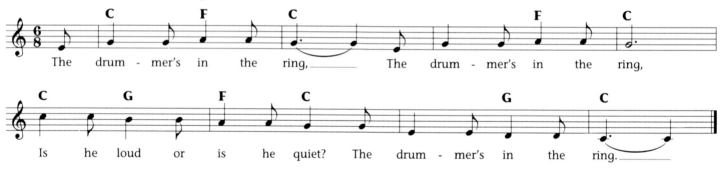

The drum - mer's in the ring,___ The drum - mer's in the ring,

Is he loud or is he quiet? The drum - mer's in the ring.___

24 Listen, children - Mary, Mary quite contrary

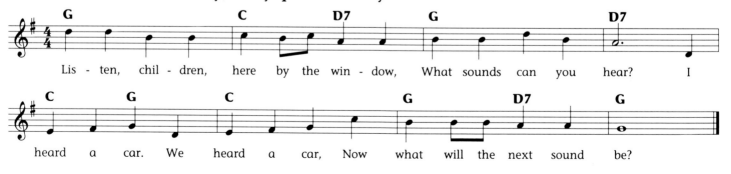

Lis - ten, chil - dren, here by the win - dow, What sounds can you hear? I

heard a car. We heard a car, Now what will the next sound be?

25 Mrs Bear - Oats and beans and barley grow

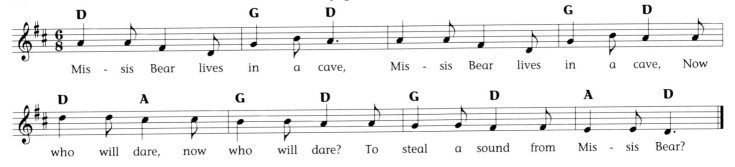

Mis - sis Bear lives in a cave, Mis - sis Bear lives in a cave, Now

who will dare, now who will dare? To steal a sound from Mis - sis Bear?

26 Make your sound like mine - Do you know the muffin man?

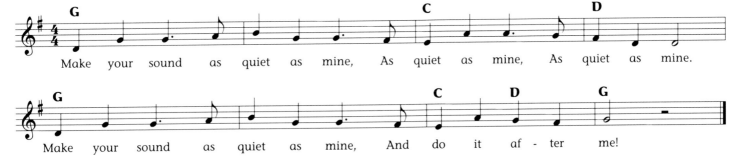

Make your sound as quiet as mine, As quiet as mine, As quiet as mine.

Make your sound as quiet as mine, And do it af - ter me!

27 Some sounds are short - Pease pudding hot

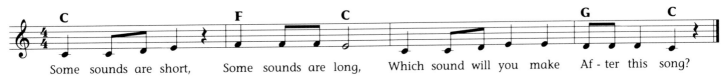

Some sounds are short, Some sounds are long, Which sound will you make Af - ter this song?

28 One sound can be heard - One man went to mow

One sound can be heard, When we sing to - ge - ther. One sound can be heard, When we sing to - ge - ther.

29 Clap your hands and wiggle your fingers - Bobby Shaftoe

Clap your hands and wig - gle your fin - gers, Clap your hands and wig - gle your fin - gers,

Clap your hands and wig - gle your fin - gers, Now we've made a pat - tern.

30 Hold a stick in this hand - Sing a song of sixpence

Hold a stick in this hand, Hold a stick in that,

Put them both to - ge - ther, Let them tap, tap, tap.

Tap them near the cei - ling, Tap them near the ground,

Tap them just in front of you, Then gen - tly put them down.

31 Clap hands, follow me - Skip to my loo

Clap hands fol - low me, Clap hands fol - low me,

Clap hands fol - low me, Who will be lea - der next time?

32 Hand upon your head - Jelly on the plate

Hand u - pon your head, Hand u - pon your head, Up and down, Up and down, Hand u - pon your head.

33 Round the ring - Here we go round the mulberry bush

So - phie is walk - ing round the ring, Round the ring, round the ring,

So - phie is walk - ing round the ring, What will she choose to play?

34 Stick-tapping - The wheels on the bus

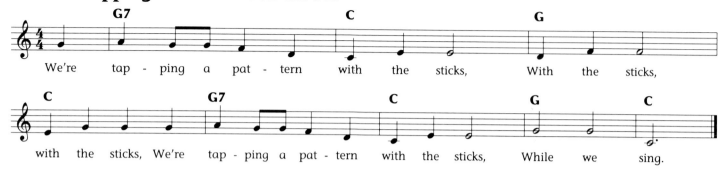

We're tap - ping a pat - tern with the sticks, With the sticks,

with the sticks, We're tap - ping a pat - tern with the sticks, While we sing.

35 Tap your name - Hot cross buns

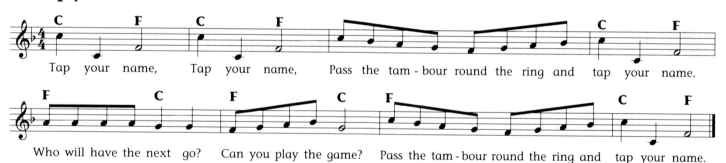

Tap your name, Tap your name, Pass the tam - bour round the ring and tap your name.

Who will have the next go? Can you play the game? Pass the tam - bour round the ring and tap your name.

36 I can play you my sound - Ring a ring o' roses

I can play you my sound, I can play you my sound, I play, I play, We all play now.

37 Do you know the colours? - Oranges and lemons

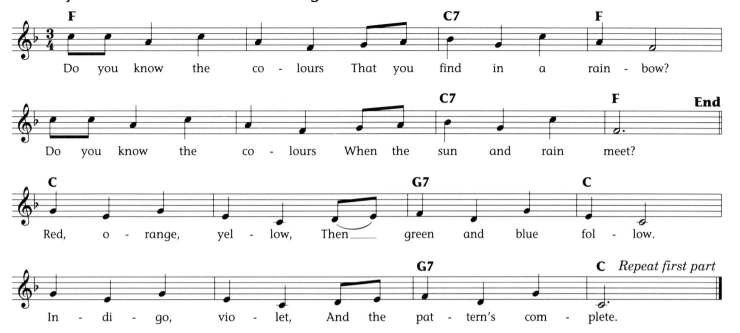

F   C7   F

Do you know the co - lours That you find in a rain - bow?

C7   F   **End**

Do you know the co - lours When the sun and rain meet?

C   G7   C

Red, o - range, yel - low, Then green and blue fol - low.

G7   C *Repeat first part*

In - di - go, vio - let, And the pat - tern's com - plete.

Index of first lines

More classroom music from A & C Black . . .

High Low Dolly Pepper
A resource book of poems, songs, activities and
games to help you explore music with young
children.

Game-songs with Prof Dogg's Troupe
44 songs and games with activities — the best
ever and most popular book of new action
songs for young children.

Okki-tokki-unga
All the traditional and best-loved action songs
in one hilariously illustrated collection.

The Singing Sack
28 stories from around the world, which each
contain a simple song for children to sing as the
story unfolds. All the songs are recorded on a
companion cassette.

Count Me In
44 songs and rhymes — both traditional and
new — which teach children about numbers.

For further details of these and all our titles, please write to: A & C Black, P.O. Box 19, Huntingdon, Cambs PE19 3SF.